Shut Up And Listen!

(The World According To Me)

Carl Robinson

authorHOUSE®

AuthorHouse™
1663 Liberty Drive
Bloomington, IN 47403
www.authorhouse.com
Phone: 1-800-839-8640

First published by AuthorHouse 11/9/2010

ISBN: 978-1-4520-8613-2 (sc)
ISBN: 978-1-4520-8614-9 (e)

Library of Congress Control Number: 2010915399

Printed in the United States of America

This book is printed on acid-free paper.

Certain stock imagery © Thinkstock.

To Ashleigh, Monster, J-Lo, Alec and Ollie-Vee:
I hope you will still have the liberty to
read this in your later years.
I love you!

To Nicky...
The woman of my dreams!
I love you!

Table of Contents

Introduction

"The secret to success is to offend the greatest number of people…"
-George Bernard Shaw

I'm hoping Mr. Shaw's theory holds true for me. Success means money and money means power. I like that. And if I can achieve that by offending those who need to be offended, then the lottery has been won. (Literally and figuratively speaking).

I consider myself to be a very patriotic individual. I love America and all that it stands for. I also believe in full disclosure. I won't pretend to be "unbiased" nor will I adhere to any "politically correct" jargon. I am a traditionalist. I am a conservative. I am a Republican. I am an unashamed Capitalist and an unapologetic Christian.

I'm sure there will be plenty of people who will disagree with my views. But then again, nobody's perfect. America has fallen and she has fallen hard. Of course, it doesn't help when you have people such as Mr. Obama, Nancy Pelosi and Harry Reid, pushing her with all their might. They are quickly leading us down a Socialist path and are determined to undermine everything our Founding Fathers established and fought for.

These are my views and they are based on my own personal experiences and personal biases. I use facts and figures, here and there, to support what I am saying, as any good author will do. But I try not to clutter up the pages with too many numbers. Numbers don't lie but they sure can be manipulated. I'm much more concerned with addressing the *issue*.

Although I never go out of my way to offend people, it is a given that it is going to happen. When you discuss religion and politics, somebody is going to get hurt. To be blunt: that's not my problem. I tell it the way I see it and I am entitled to my opinion just like anyone else.

Just keep one thing in mind as you read this book…

The truth hurts.

Part I:
The Book

"It's just a matter of time until the rest of the world
comes around to my way of thinking…"
-Carl Robinson

Chapter One:
Celebrities

Why is that celebrities think that fame equals intelligence? These are people who can rarely manage their own lives and yet they try to influence me?

There are a whole slew of actors and musicians who oppose the War in Iraq. They cite the loss of American lives as part of their reasoning. Which is true...war does cost lives. But what about the thousands of lives that had been taken under the dictatorship of Saddam Hussein? Do those lives not count because they were not Americans? That seems to be the logic of these celebrities. They seem to conveniently forget the inhumanities the Iraqi people had suffered.

A lot of celebrities claim we didn't try hard enough to find a peaceful resolution. That's a lie. We DID try to resolve the issue peacefully. It didn't work. Saddam Hussein would not cooperate. As far as I'm concerned, we gave Saddam too many chances. We allowed him more than enough time to dispose of any evidence of WMD's. We did the right thing by taking him out of power. The evidence is in the fact that Iraq now has free elections. Or look back at the footage of the Iraqi people tearing down Saddam Hussein's statue. How can you not think that the world is a better place without Saddam Hussein in power?

These celebrities would deny others the very freedom that allows them (the celebrities) to protest the war. They would deny these people the freedom that they take for granted. The Dixie Chicks even went so far as to use their right to free speech to lash out against President Bush while they were performing in another country. (We see what happened to their career). These people use the First Amendment to speak out against a war that has liberated an entire nation and given others the God-given right to free speech. How noble is that?

I also love these commercials on TV where celebrities encourage me, and actually try to instruct me, on how to be a good parent! It's laughable but it's also insulting. You have someone who has no regard for anything they are preaching about. These are people who laugh about their multiple three-month marriages, shrug off their liaisons with prostitutes and repeatedly have to be checked in to the Betty Ford clinic.

And they're trying to tell *me* how to be a better parent?

It's an ego trip. It puts them in this angelic light and it makes for good publicity. Their sincerity begins and ends with the cue card they're reading from.

Actors should just do what they do best: be good actors. They should stick to reading lines that are written by other people. There is a reason why their lines are written for them.

Chapter Two:
The War In Iraq

A few years back when the war in Iraq first started, there was a narrow-minded, politically motivated tactic that was being utilized by the Democrats. They sought to demonize not only the war itself, but also anyone who supported the war and even going so far as to disrespect the men and women that are serving.

What was funniest about it all was the way they kept switching sides. They obviously had the "John Kerry" syndrome. They supported the war at first but when it started to become unpopular, they tried to portray themselves as opponents of the war. They had the exact same intelligence information in front of them that President Bush had, and THEY voted to go to war.

The Democrats stepped up their efforts to demonize the war when no WMD's were found. Keep in mind that the UN had given Saddam Hussein more than ample time to hide and destroy any evidence, so of course we didn't find any! Despite the "absence" of WMD's, there were plenty of other justifiable reasons to invade Iraq. The best reason was to remove Saddam Hussein. By doing this, we created a beacon of hope for the rest of the Middle East. We are introducing a Democracy, and hopefully Christianity, in an area that desperately needs it. In my opinion, we shouldn't have stopped in Iraq. We should have taken Iran as well.

And what about the people of Iraq? Hadn't they suffered enough under Saddam Hussein? Everyone is entitled to inalienable rights that most Americans take for granted. Most of our liberal brethren tend to believe that these rights are reserved for only a certain select few. Saddam Hussein utilized rape and torture rooms. Imagine being a woman that is raped day after day for the twisted amusement of a demented dictator. Or imagine being a man and being forced to watch as your wife is raped day after day. Not to mention the chemical weapons that he used on his own people. Why exactly did the Liberals oppose this war?!

Another issue raised by the Liberals is that the U.S. lead Coalition strike was a pre-emptive one. I say...so what? That's not always a bad thing. In fact, in this particular case it was a *good* thing. It was better to take him out than to wait for him to show up at our front door. (Does anyone remember 9/11?). No one worries much about the crazy guy with a gun that lives a thousand miles from nowhere. But we panic when suddenly he's standing on our front porch with a gun pointed at our head. The problem is, by that time it's too late.

Another favorite argument the Liberals used was "War for Oil". Even if that was part of our reasoning, it's *good* reasoning. We need to protect something that we clearly have a vested interest in. We wouldn't have to import so much oil if the Liberals would allow us to tap into our own resources. The liberals won't let us tap into the abundance of oil we have in Alaska because it might upset a few caribou. Offshore drilling is nearly non-existent, even though we have tremendous amounts of oil at our disposal there as well. There haven't been any new refineries built since the 1970's! The Liberals have created this problem for us and yet they don't want us to protect the only viable option we have left. I thought these people were supposed to be intelligent...

Even so, the people of Iraq are now free to pursue a democracy and they no longer have to live in fear of a tyrannical dictator. Who cares what the Liberals think? Whether we went there for oil or to sell

Tupperware, the end result is the same: Saddam Hussein is no longer in power.

If I was an Iraqi, who had known nothing but fear and tyranny, and then someone comes along and liberates me and eliminates that tyranny, I'm not going to question *why* he did it.

I'm just glad he *did*.

Chapter Three:
France, Germany and the U.N.

Let me start off by saying that I once visited France and I found it to be a very nice place to visit. It's a very beautiful country and a profound culture. I spent two weeks in and around Paris and still couldn't cover everything I would have liked to have seen. Most of the people I encountered were very nice and most of them spoke English, which was very fortunate for me. Granted I had taken two years of French in High School but my understanding and vocabulary was very limited.

With that said, I have to say that despite the pleasantries that came with my trip, France is a very conceited and presumptuous nation. France, Germany and the U.N. wanted no part of the war to liberate Iraq. But once the war was over they wanted to be a part of the rebuilding of Iraq. What gives them the right? They didn't earn that privilege. Sometimes the United States is too diplomatic...too nice. We didn't need their help liberating Iraq and we certainly didn't need their help rebuilding Iraq. I would have excluded them from having *any* part of the restoration.

The U.N. is a big waste. It's a think-tank for Socialistic policy and oppression. This idea of a "one world government" titillates them to no end. They would love to do away with the Second Amendment, not to mention Christianity. Private ownership would be abolished as well.

Our involvement is a big mistake. It's obvious that we don't need the U.N., the U.N. needs US! The Coalition of Nations that fought for Iraqi freedom proves that we don't need the U.N. And I can think of nothing more insulting to our Armed Forces than to have to have "approval" from the U.N. and the European Nations in order to defend our allies and our interests abroad. Yet our current state of mind is just that. Mr. Obama would never take any real military action without consulting the U.N. and all of our "friends" in Europe. The proof for that is the "stern letter" he wrote to North Korea after they fired a missile across the Sea of Japan. In fact, I wouldn't be surprised if he didn't first seek the approval of at least five Muslim nations as well. What happened to the days of Ronald Reagan? When America was strong and stood for Democracy and Freedom.

France, of all nations, should know the value of being liberated from tyranny. When you consider that they have been defeated, humiliated and occupied in both World Wars (and then rescued by the United States), they should have been the first to step up to rid the world of another dictator. But since it wasn't France that was suffering and being held captive, they didn't see the need to take action. They didn't find it to be the "moral" thing to do. It was "unfounded" and "pre-emptive" from their point of view. I have a feeling that if it *would* have been France that was being tormented by a ruthless dictator and the United States came to their aid (once again), the word "pre-emptive" would never have entered the picture.

I think most of the French citizens supported their government's stance on the issue. And for that, I consider them to be cowardly, pre-sumptuous, arrogant and self-centered. And those are the nice things I have to say about them. When a nation needed to be liberated from a tyrant they wanted no part of it, even though they had once faced the same peril only decades ago.

But remember how France responded to the situation in Haiti not long after the United States invaded Iraq? They criticized us for inter-vening in Iraq without U.N. support, but then turned around and did the same thing in Haiti! I think that's called a double standard.

Random Thought Number One: Lobster - Cockroach of the Sea

I find it revolting that people actually eat lobster and crab and shrimp. You're basically eating marine cockroaches.

I think Gene Simmons summed it up best when he said if aliens ever landed on our planet, you could walk over to them, scratch their backs and lobsters would fall off. I firmly believe that there is life on other planets and lobsters are proof of that. They are most certainly alien life forms that have successfully inhabited our planet.

And you're *eating* them!

Chapter Four:

"CNN" Music

As I'm writing this book I'm listening to Elvis. It's great music to write to. It's great music no matter what I'm doing. It isn't too cerebral and the "message" songs are far and few. It's what it's supposed to be: escapism.

There was a dark period in music during the 1990's. It was the worst time in music history since the late 1960's. I remember being in college at the time and everyone was listening to Grunge and Alternative music. College Radio was at it's peak. People would laugh at me because I was still listening to some of the music from the 1980's and 1970's. Not that I was in complete nostalgic mode. I've always kept up on the latest music whether I like it or not. I love music and it's a big part of my life. My friends are amazed at the amount of music trivia that I know. They are even more amazed at my collection. At last count, I have well over 250,000 songs on my hard drive.

I certainly enjoyed some of the music that was coming out at the time. I thought Nirvana was interesting but I certainly shed no tears when Kurt Cobain shot himself. In fact, I called him a loser and coward. He left his child and wife due to his own selfishness. But that's beside the point. I really thought Soundgarden was excellent and Smashing Pumpkins were brilliant! But on the whole, it was a horrific time for music. All the fun had been taken out of it. There was no entertainment aspect and all the songs were depressing. Who wants to listen to that? Not me. I referred to it as "CNN" music, meaning that most of the songs were news headlines set to drop-D tuning.

Music is supposed to be an escape. It's supposed to take you *away* from all the troubles of the world. If I want a depressing message, I'll turn on the news…although it would not be CNN (Clinton News Network). If I want to be educated on a topic then I will read a book or search online. I don't need a musician telling me how I should change my ways and accept a new lifestyle. If you want to save whales and hug trees then do it. But don't try to demonize me because I eat Angus Burgers from McDonald's (that makes me cruel to animals) while you support and condone abortion (that makes *you* cruel to babies!).

Rock and roll is supposed to be about being free, believing in your-self and leaving your cares behind. When you take that away you lose the essence of what rock and roll is all about.

Bands like Pearl Jam and Rage Against The Machine are worst. They sing nothing but "message" songs about how the "white man" is the oppressor and "everything is terrible". Can you cut out the "poor me" attitude? In this day and age I would much rather be a minority than to be white. The only discrimination I see is Illegal Immigration and Affirmative Action (more on those later). Listening to a bunch of whiny guys talking about how bad everything is just isn't convincing when you know they are making millions of dollars doing what they love.

Back to Kurt Cobain. Everyone tried to portray him as a cultural icon. And worthless magazines like Rolling Stone only perpetuated this delusional ideal. The guy was talented and wrote some cool tunes but that's really about it. He did nothing more for me. He looked like a bum and the stage shows were boring. Again, the antithesis of rock and roll.

A rock concert should be exciting. It should be a big show. If I just want to hear some good music then I'll stay home and listen to my iPod. But when I go to a concert I'm not just bringing my ears. I'm also bringing my eyes. So give me more for my money! Dress the part! Rock stars are supposed to *look* like rock stars! They shouldn't look like they just rolled out of bed or like they just came from the unemployment line. Take cue from great bands like KISS, Motley Crue and even the Beatles.

It's ok to sing a few message songs. It shouldn't always be mindless escapism. Elvis is *the* premier artist of the century. Some of his biggest hits were songs regarding social issues of the day. Songs like "In The Ghetto" and "If I Can Dream" were about racial equality. But a majority of his tunes had no real message. It was just fun music to listen to. And when you went to an Elvis concert, you were going to see a *show*! He gave his audience bang for the buck. I never got to see Elvis because I was only 3 when he died. But I've seen KISS at least 15 times in the past 10 years and it never grows old. They continue to put on the Hottest Show on Earth (to coin the name of their upcoming U.S. tour).

Fortunately most of the bands that came out during the 90's have broken up or been dropped by their labels. I remember how those bands used to make fun of the "hair" bands and now the "hair" bands are actually doing better than the alternative bands. What comes around goes around…

Thank God KISS reunited in 1996 and brought fun and showmanship back to rock and roll. They brought back the big stages, the rock star look and attitude, and the big shows. KISS opened the doors for the 80's bands to reunite and put together package tours that filled arenas and amphitheaters again. And the alternative bands were left in the dust.

That's called karma.

Chapter Five:
Affirmative Action

It is absolutely insulting to anyone's intelligence to see an employer with the phrase "We are an Equal Opportunity/Affirmative Action Employer" on their applications for employment. What a contradiction! How can you be "equal opportunity" and "affirmative action" at the same time? You can't! If you were truly an "equal opportunity" employer then you would not subscribe to the reverse discrimination that is "affirmative action".

I know I will take some heat for this and I'm sure I'll be accused of being racist, blah blah blah. But the fact of the matter is, affirmative action is the equivalent of reverse discrimination. In it's formative years it was used to level the playing field. But it has outlived it's usefulness. Fortunately I live in a state that voted to end affirmative action. But there are plenty of states that are still saddled with this atrocity.

I won't deny nor defend the terrible travesties that befell minorities of years ago. Slavery was/is an absolute abomination in any sense. It is a dark chapter in our great nation's history and it should never be forgotten or forsaken. But slavery has been abolished for over 100 years. The civil rights amendment for over 40 years.

No one should ever forget that the Native Americans were here first. The Europeans were sometimes terrible and ruthless in their dealings with Native Americans. Again, it's a dark chapter in the history of our great nation. But it was over 100 years ago.

No one can deny that Chinese immigrants were subjected to unethical and unfair labor practices. They were underpaid, ridiculed and under appreciated. But that was also over 100 years ago.

This isn't to say that racism doesn't still exist because it does. However, what most people fail to recognize is that *everybody* is guilty of it. Not just white people. As I stated earlier, it's much better to be a minority in America than to be white in America. Only in America can you have Black Entertainment Television or Miss Black America but if you started a White Entertainment Television channel or a Miss White America pageant, you would be labeled as racist. Only in America is it ok to have certain student loans made available *only* to minorities.

Affirmative Action is no longer needed. It only serves to appease the masses. It calls for unfair advantages and quotas that lean in the favor of minorities. For example, if you apply for a job with any of the auto-makers you have to pass an entrance exam, so to speak. You have to obtain a certain score to even be considered for the position you're applying for. However, if you're a minority you don't have to score as high as a white person. How fair is that? To me, *that* is racist. *That* is discrimination. But it's perfectly acceptable because no one will stand up and try to change it! White people are afraid to question it because they will be labeled as racist and most of the minorities are too content with accepting entitlements. There are exceptions to every rule of course. Bill Cosby is a huge proponent of black people accepting responsibility. His commentaries on "quit blaming white people" are disturbingly accurate.

Diversity is the backbone of our nation. It's the culmination of culture that has made America the greatest nation on Earth. As a Christian I am especially aware of equality and what it means. God created all of us. No one is better than the person next to him. Therefore, I think that jobs should go to the person best qualified for the job. It should be based on education, experience, compatibility and moral stature. In other words: qualifications. But yet, if a white person and a black person apply for the same job, there is a very good chance that the black person will be hired, solely because of quotas and affirmative action.

The idea of restitution and "charity" would once have been insulting to a Native American. Now it's a way of life. Casinos have turned a once proud nation into a bunch of drunken, gambling fools. Again, there are exceptions and I realize I'm painting in broad strokes. But more and more I see Native Americans who do nothing more than collect their checks off the Casinos that, for "some" reason, only Native Americans are allowed to have. Again, it's an outdated idea that perpetuates a reverse discriminatory ideology. But only in America is it acceptable.

The United States makes it possible for Chinese immigrants to open new businesses here and not have to pay taxes. And when that person's tax free period is about to end, he can transfer the business to a relative and they will enjoy a tax free business. But yet there are no amenities like that for me or anyone else because we're not Chinese. We're just tax-paying citizens is all.

No matter how you look at it, affirmative action is reverse discrimination, and it's wrong. Quotas, reparations and tax-breaks based on race only serve to further divide us culturally. A nation will only truly be diversified and *equal* when all unfair practices are abolished.

Chapter Six:
Abortion

No one can deny that life begins at conception. If a fetus wasn't alive, it could not grow. So doing anything which ends or "terminates" that life would be, by definition, killing (or murdering) it. To end a life is to kill it. No matter how you try to define it or dress it up, it is what it is.

Liberals want to portray this as a woman's issue. They try to tell us that it's a woman's body and she should have the right to do with it as she pleases. But they are neglecting a very important point. The fetus is NOT a part of the woman's body such as her appendix. You remove an appendix and it no longer functions. When you remove a baby from it's womb it will survive and grow. An appendix will have the same genetic make-up and blood type as the person it belongs to. A fetus has it's own unique genetic make-up and may not even have the same blood type as the mother. So although the Liberals would like to classify abortion as a "woman's choice" or a woman's issue…They're wrong.

It's a human issue. It's strikes the very core of what our moral principles should dictate. Yes, it's the woman who carries the baby but that's through no choice of our own. It's not as though women volunteered for the position. It's simply what God intended. And who are you to play God and decide who should live or die? Accept responsibility for your actions. You decided to have sex and you certainly knew what the end

17

result could be. We teach our children to be responsible and we should certainly hold ourselves to that same standard. On a whim a woman can decide that the life she carries within her is an inconvenience and terminate that life. The life she has within her is completely innocent and has done nothing wrong. It simply becomes a victim of circumstance. As Mike Huckabee so accurately points out, the womb should be the safest place for a new life. But as of late it has become the most dangerous place for new life.

Liberals defend abortion to no end. Ann Coulter calls it their "religion" and I must say that I agree. Liberals look for new ways all the time to further advance and promote their abortionist agenda. Bill Clinton tried to legalize RU486. When that failed the Liberals simply turned to embryonic stem cell research (more on that later). But before that, they pushed for partial birth abortion. Liberals are intent on making abortion legal on all levels, no matter at what term in the pregnancy.

The media, which is blatantly liberally biased, continues to label those who are for abortion as "pro-choice" and those who are against it as "anti-choice". That might not seem like a big deal but it really is. It's the connotation that the prefix "anti" carries. And when you throw out a term such as "anti-choice" it makes it sound as though those of us against abortion are against personal choice and personal liberties. It's an inaccurate label but the media will never use the term "pro-life" because if they did they would expose the "pro-choice" advocates for what they really are: "anti-life". But since this is MY book and I can use whatever terms I want to, I will use the labels "pro-life" and "anti-life" because I feel they are much more accurate terms.

There are many arguments that the anti-life people use to defend their abortionist agenda. Some of them are pretty creative so I will give them credit for originality. But when you really break down their arguments you see that there is no real substance. Their arguments are based on misnomers, half-truths and outright lies. And when you base your arguments on those pillars it eventually comes crashing down. So let's take a look at their reasoning for defending abortion and break it down and expose it for the immorality that it truly is...

Some argue that the mother may be too young or uneducated or unemployed (or all of the above) and therefore cannot care for the baby. My first reaction to that is to say that the girl shouldn't have been having sex then. But since she (and an equally irresponsible young man) decided to have sex anyway, they should be willing and ready to accept the responsibility of their actions. I am willing to admit that a 14 year old girl is not the ideal parent. But there are other options besides abortion and the most practical and loving one is adoption. There are millions of couples who cannot have their own children and would love to adopt. It's a slap in the face when a loving couple cannot conceive, for whatever reason, but yet you have all these young girls who are having multiple abortions. Abortion is wrong, unethical, irresponsible, immoral and disgusting, and to use it as a form of birth control is the epitome of evil.

It would also help if these boys, who feel man enough to have sex, would also feel man enough to step up and be responsible fathers. It would also help if parents would be PARENTS again instead of trying to be their kids best friend. If you have a 13 year old that is having sex you are just as much to blame. Do your job and be a responsible parent, and your kids will grow up to do the same.

The anti-life people also like to use rape as an argument for abortion. The chances of getting pregnant during a rape is almost non-existent. The conditions for conceiving are quite staggering. Everything has to be lined up just right. It's a wonder that women can get pregnant at all if you really look at what all has to take place in order to conceive! And I'm sure everyone would agree that rape is NOT the ideal condition to conceive. Most sources state that between 1 and 5% of women raped will end up pregnant. Those are extremely low numbers. But granted, it DOES happen.

But let me ask you this…does that mean the CHILD should die? None of us can control or be responsible for the conditions for which we were conceived but most of us are glad to be alive. This is still an unborn baby that will grow to be your own child. How could you not love it no matter what circumstance the child came to be? Instead, we abort the child and give the criminal, guilty of rape, life in prison where he gets a free education, free cable TV and room and board. Where is the justice in that? And again, adoption is still the better option. If you truly would not be able to love your child because of the horrible conditions from which he was conceived, then let someone else love that child.

As a person who is pro-life I do not like that my tax dollars will soon be used to fund abortions (under the new Obamacare plan…more on that later). If a person chooses to kill their unborn child then they should have to use their own money to do so. I want no part of it nor should I have to be.

Liberals place no value on life other than their own. Liberals have a hierarchy and if you don't meet their criteria, they simply deem you disposable. Does this sound familiar? It should. Hitler held the same belief. Since Liberals are Socialists and Socialists are basically a "diet" Communist, my argument isn't too off base. The liberal anti-life people use physical and mental disabilities to justify abortion as well. I mean, who wants a retarded child or a kid with cerebral palsy right? That's the mindset of these people. Now obviously no one WANTS to have a child with any physical or mental affliction. The difference between liberal socialists and conservative Christians is that, although we wouldn't hope for a child with any sort of impairment, we would love our child just as much even if he did. Liberals would simply have an abortion. Too much of an inconvenience to take care of these kids for the rest of their lives. It doesn't say much about you as a person if you cannot love your child because of a physical or mental impairment. These kids have just as much a right to live as anyone else. Again I turn to Mike Huckabee, who accurately stated, that a society that kills it's children will soon have this same generation grow up to deem US "disposable" in our old age. It's called euthanasia (another cornerstone of the Liberal agenda…just refer to Obamacare for further proof).

There are millions of children who are born with some sort of physical or mental impairment and they all make a huge impact on our lives. They enrich our lives because they remind us how fortunate the rest of us are. They keep us from taking anything for granted. They make us appreciate life so much more. There are numerous individuals who have been born with disabilities that have made huge contributions to society.

Helen Keller was both deaf and blind (although, she is responsible for the ACLU so I'm not sure she is the best example to use).

I have an uncle who is pro-life but feels the government should not dictate whether a woman has an abortion or not. Being a conservative Republican, I can certainly appreciate smaller government and less government control (something the Liberals obviously ignore). But the government does have certain obligations to it's people. Namely, to protect it's citizens. Whether that be in time of war or from being gunned down in your own neighborhood, the government is supposed to protect my right to live. And that should extend to those who are not yet born, but are still clearly "alive". From the point of conception until the time I die, the government is charged with the responsibility to keep me safe from foreign invaders, street thugs and even my own mother if need be.

If you consider yourself a Christian I'm not sure how you can be "pro-choice"? Liberals like to perpetuate the misnomer of "separation of church and state" and unfortunately a good portion of the population has bought into it. The fact of the matter is, our Founding Fathers never intended for our government to operate outside of God. Everything that forms the foundation of our country is based on God. If you consider yourself a Christian then you should adamantly be speaking out against abortion and electing officials who are pro-life, because it IS the government's job to protect the lives of the unborn as well.

How can a society that is supposed to be civilized condone something so barbaric? It's just another example of the moral decline of Western Civilization. And it breeds in the form of liberal propaganda.

Random Thought Number Two: Hulk Hogan

Professional wrestling is the ultimate in entertainment. When describing wrestling, a lot of people will throw around the term "fake". But I tell you that wrestling is not only real, it's actually a lot more honest than most other sports. The athletes are phenomenal. To be able to take those hits and know how to do them without getting hurt is an amazing talent.

I must say that I am disappointed in the WWE. Vince McMahon refuses to admit that Hulk Hogan is the reason his organization is in the position it is today. The WWE is less about wrestling and more about soap opera storylines and naked women.

The reason wrestling became so popular can be summed up in two words: Hulk Hogan. He defines and epitomizes what made wrestling great. The only time I will watch wrestling is if Hulk Hogan is on. TNA made the best decision in their entire history by signing Hulk Hogan to their organization.

It won't be long until the WWE is a distant second to TNA.

Chapter Seven:
Capital Punishment

I support capital punishment. For various reasons. Why should a criminal guilty of murder live a life of luxury at my expense?

Prison is almost better than being free. You get free room and board, cable television, a gym membership, free college education and much more. All of this is paid for with our tax dollars. That's your "punishment" for having committed a terrible crime.

It's quite simple. If you kill someone, you deserve to die. It's not about revenge. And it's not about "an eye for an eye". It's simply the best deterrent to repeat offending. If you're dead, you can no longer kill or rape.

Through capital punishment we would save tax dollars. People talk about how prisoners sentenced to death actually cost more than prisoners who are housed for life. And I have to admit that that is true. However, if you were to limit the number of appeals then capital punishment would be far more cost effective.

What is mind boggling to me are the liberals who support abortion but are against capital punishment. It's ok to kill an innocent unborn baby that has never done anything wrong, but it's NOT ok to kill someone who is guilty of murder? That only makes sense in a liberal's mind.

Liberals believe that criminals should be rehabilitated and given another chance. Which is ironic since the person who was murdered will never get another chance.

Prisoners will complain about their living conditions. They should just be thankful that they ARE living. They don't deserve to be alive. They are criminals and they should be treated as such. Cable TV and weight rooms should not be provided. These are NOT necessities.

Liberals like to spend a lot of time trying to figure criminals out. They want to know why the criminal did what he did. In reality, they are looking for excuses for the criminal's behavior. Criminals like to blame society. It was society's fault for their criminal activities. And liberals not only buy into it, they perpetuate it and force down people's throats. Doesn't anyone take responsibility for their actions anymore? There is a lot to be said for holding yourself accountable.

If your life is a mess then do something about it. If you do poorly in school or at your job, then don't blame your teacher or your boss. And if you kill someone that is *your fault*. YOU made that decision. Don't try to blame your parents or your friends or the kid in school that made fun of you because you didn't have any friends. You have the right to be held accountable for your actions.

Chapter Eight:
Illegal Immigrants

The notion of paying fair wages and providing insurance benefits to illegal immigrants is preposterous. They are here *illegally.* Hence the term *illegal immigrant.* You do not reward illegal behavior with better wages and insurance benefits. You escort them out of the country and return them to their homeland.

The most obvious case of illegal immigration is with Mexico. I understand *why* Mexicans want to live in America. Even if they are only making $2.00 an hour, it's still better than living in Mexico. However, they are here illegally, which presents several problems.

If you allow Mexicans to live here illegally then you have to allow every other illegal immigrant from every other country to live here also.

You have liberal Democrats who want to provide illegal immigrants with insurance benefits, welfare benefits and higher wages. That costs money. And who pays for that? Those of us that are here legally and pay taxes.

If companies can hire illegal immigrants to work for $2.00 an hour (and be paid "under the table"), it drives down wages for everyone else. A lot of liberals claim that illegal immigrants are doing the jobs that no one else will do. I guess that's their way of justifying the criminal behavior. I'm sure I could find plenty of U.S. citizens that would be willing to do the work. Especially when our unemployment rate is at 10%.

The recent passage of Arizona's immigration law has been the subject of controversy. Personally, I think it's only about time. Other states should pass similar laws. The American people have the right to be protected and since the Federal government isn't going to do anything about it, then I guess it's up to the states.

The fact of the matter is that the United States is becoming overpopulated. And the tax burden on Americans (especially the middle class) is excruciating. Illegal immigration contributes to both of these factors. The reality is that the U.S. needs to end ALL immigration for about ten years to allow the population to acclimate.

Border patrol needs to be drastically stepped-up. The military needs to have a much stronger presence along the U.S.-Mexico border, along with a security fence along the entire border as well. Mr. Obama insults the American people's intelligence by sending 2,500 military persons to the border. He truly thinks the American public is a bunch of idiots.

America needs to shut her borders if she hopes to sustain her current population and promote economic growth.

Part II:
A Compilation of My
Various Articles

(Previously found in my newsletter, "The Voice of Reason"

"Once you get what you want, that's when you've got something to lose..."

Chapter Nine:
America and Her Parallels to Ancient Israel

Recently while reading the book of Isaiah, I have noticed some alarming passages that demonstrate the rise and fall of Israel, that now seem to be coming to fruition in America. Of course, Israel's history is told throughout many books in the Bible and I noticed the parallels early on. But only recently did it strike me as imminent.

Without getting too political (which is a challenge for me), you can see that the current state that this country is in is very similar to Israel just before the exile to Babylon. Israel was God's chosen nation. Israel was to set an example for all the other nations of the world. In fact, the Bible says that Israel was the envy of all other nations. Israel was given God's blessings. She was given the best of everything (the land of milk and honey). But Israel grew arrogant. Not arrogant as far as a conceit toward other nations but more so from within. Israel's leaders were guilty of cheating the poor, the elderly and widows. They allowed the worship of idols and false gods. They offered sub-par sacrifices. They desecrated the Temple.

Israel was given several warnings by various prophets. But the leaders and the people were so arrogant that they believed that not even God could take it away from them. When Israel was near it's end, the people did not restore their faith in God. They instead called upon their false gods and sought the help of foreign nations. But it was futile. Israel was destroyed and it's people were lead into exile. It was only much later that God allowed his chosen people to return to their homeland.

If you look at America and it's history, you will see the parallels. I honestly believe that God chose America to be the beacon of light for the rest of the world. God blessed our country from the very beginning. Even though our army was much smaller than Britain's, we still gained our independence. The same held true for Israel. They fought already established nations and still took the land of Canaan.

America, in her very short history, became the sole world power. Other countries are envious of what America has and what America stands for. That is the reason for the attacks of 9/11. And even though America is the sole world power, never has she used her strength to invade peaceful nations. She has never sought to be an empire. In fact, America helps many nations and rarely gets anything in return.

America's weakness comes from within. Just like ancient Israel, our leaders have allowed the disintegration of the foundation God wanted us to build upon. Pornography is accepted as freedom of speech. Abortion is a "woman's right". Euthanasia is disguised as "dieing with dignity". God has been taken out of our public schools and government buildings. We are allowing our leaders to lead us down the same path that Israel followed. And we are either too blind, or too passive, to stand up and take our nation back.

Again, without getting too political, the fault certainly lies with every individual who does nothing to change this, but the catalyst for this lies solely with the liberals of our present times. It's the liberals who want to take God out of the Pledge of Allegiance. It's the liberals who took the Ten Commandments out of government buildings. It's the liberals who still defend abortion. It's the liberals who want "holiday trees" and "happy holidays" instead of "Christmas trees" and "Merry Christmas".

The point is this: we are making the same mistakes that Israel made and if we don't make some changes soon, we will suffer the same fate. We are meant to be the nation that inspires other nations to be better.

To aspire for more. To reap the benefits of Democracy. It's not too late…!

I honestly believe that our current administration, headed by Mr. Obama, is leading us down a path of certain doom. The erosion of Judeo-Christian principles will most certainly be our undoing. But again…it's not too late! I encourage anyone who loves America and appreciates the foundation in which she was built upon, to vote for conservative leaders in 2010. Our Senate and House of Representatives are filled with a majority of liberals who are very close to passing even more liberal, Godless policies. Our fight to take America back starts there. But it doesn't end there. 2012 is the next presidential election and I encourage conservatives to turn out in record numbers. My faith is with God, my hope is with Mike Huckabee.

In the meantime, I encourage my fellow conservatives to get involved. Voting is only one aspect. Making financial contributions is another. But writing to your elected officials, believe it or not, goes a long way. Spread the Word to anyone who will listen. When people put their faith in God and live by his Word, our country as a whole can only prosper. The book of Isaiah details the peaks and valleys of ancient Israel. I personally am fond of Isaiah 51:4-8, and Isaiah 53.

God bless America!

Chapter Ten:
The "Sad" State of the Union

"Fairy tales come true...it can happen to you...."

And if your Barack Obama, you honestly believe you have actually accomplished something so far in your Presidency.

Obama and the Democrats passed their Socialist, abortion funding "health care" plan, despite the fact that 68% of the U.S. population did NOT want this program to pass. Who are these people working for? Certainly not *us!*

Economically speaking, unemployment is still high and the national debt is reaching record levels. But that hasn't stopped Obama from asking for more money to waste!

In the time that Mr. Obama has been "President", he has failed to pass most of his Socialist programs (thank God), he has released several criminals from Guantanamo that have taken up arms and are now shooting at us again AND we had terrorist attacks in Detroit.

This goes back to my argument way back in November of 2008 when I had stated, as many others had as well, that he was too new to the political arena. He had barely been elected a Senator and then the Democrats ran him for President. Of course, there are the obvious reasons WHY they ran Mr. Obama. Anyone who wouldn't vote for him could be labeled a racist…who would want to be labeled racist? And so the Democrats were able to "bully" people into supporting Mr. Obama.

But the balance is tipping in our favor. The American people have spoken literally and through election process. People have overwhelmingly stated that they do NOT want Obamacare. In fact, not even Mr. Obama wants Obamacare. Oh…it's ok for us "peasants" to have it i.e. be FORCED to have it, but he himself has stated that he "isn't sure" that he would accept it for himself. In fact, all the Democrats in Congress that are trying to impose this upon the American people have stated they wouldn't accept it. But the recent elections in Massachusetts and Illinois have shown that people want the Republicans back in power. I believe the remaining elections this year will continue to demonstrate that.

And 2012 will be the pinnacle of the downfall of Mr. Obama. I believe he will be a one-term President. The Republicans have been building momentum for the past year and a half. I'm still pulling for a Huckabee/Palin Ticket!

Addendum:
Ameripac broadcast the entire proceeding online (referring to the Health Care summit) and participants saw that Obama offered nothing new in a scheme that defrauds America. A snide Obama dominated and lectured, defending his plan that repackages the same approach already taken by the U.S. Senate. Americans have already rejected the scheme he did not want to discuss at all in the Latest Rasmussen Poll -- as 56% Oppose ObamaCare!!!!

Obama cut off discussion continually and said "move on" to stop the GOP from discussing anything that would make a real difference in healthcare reform.

Obama ignored the American public and Republicans as Reid threatened to implement ObamaCare using budget "reconciliation" with no final House or Senate Vote saying we have done this before and we can do it again.

Obama likes to do summits spending hours talking with cameras rolling. In January, Obama hosted 50 CEOS to talk about streamlining government operations and improve efficiency. We got a bigger government, with more employees and a record deficit.

In December, an Obama Forum on Jobs and Economic Growth, with business, labor and nonprofit leader and "thinkers" to talk about ways to get people back to work resulted in record unemployment and a shrink economy.

Obama has lied again. The nonpartisan Congressional Budget Office (CBO) cannot even score the latest ObamaCare scheme because it lacks enough detail to do so. The White House claim that the scheme will save $100 billion over 10 years and $1 Trillion over 20 years is refuted by the Wall Street Journal that estimates the bill will cost $950 billion over 10 years. We will get a tax increase to balance out Obama's scheme as more than $1,000,000,000 is needed in the next 10 years.

Democrats will shove ObamaCare down every Americans throat like it or not, it will happen and Obama is pushing it through and it must be stopped.

White House Communications Director Dan Pfeiffer said. "We took our best shot at bridging the differences." He then indicated that the White House is open to the Democrats using a parliamentary tool called "reconciliation" to pass the bill without 60 votes in the Senate, saying that the president's proposal is designed for "maximum flexibility" so that it could be attached to a budget bill as a way of averting a Republican filibuster.

Every person will be hurt with increased costs of an out of control Government Run Health Care bureaucracy taking over private insurance with Federal regulations. The scheme completely ignores and does not include sensible Republican proposals for a series of modest changes to bring down costs and improve coverage, including measures like tort reform and new freedoms for insurance companies to compete and sell policies across state lines.

(Source: GOPUSA)

Bill of Rights

Constitution

Declaration of Independence

Ronald Reagan

Chapter Eleven:
In Obama We Trust

Barack Obama has only been in office for just over a month and he has already provided me with volumes to write about. Just when you think he couldn't be any worse he surprises us! Just when you think there is no way he could be any more liberal, he ends up making Ted Kennedy sound like Ann Coulter. (I wouldn't dare say that Ted Kennedy LOOKS like Ann Coulter).

So let me run through some of the policies Mr. Obama has already implemented...

Before I get started I must relate to you something I have noticed. I don't watch a whole lot of TV so maybe this has changed. But the few times that I have seen Mr. Obama on TV he never salutes any of our military people. Again, maybe it's just been the few times I've been watching but that shouldn't matter. That should NEVER happen! This guy is our President and he won't salute the men and women that serve in our military? In my opinion, he should be impeached just for that.

Speaking of the military...one of the first atrocities Mr. Obama implemented was the closing of Guantanamo Bay. Hey...let's just let ALL the terrorists our military worked so hard to capture have their freedom! I mean...terrorists are people too, right? They should not be kept in such places. We should have rented them rooms at the Holiday

Inn. Are Liberals really this stupid? I mean, how can you be THAT incompetent and actually make it through life?

Our military people put their lives on the line every day. They do a selfless act which results in you and I having the freedoms we cherish. It's a very hard job and a very THANKLESS job at times (only because Liberals exist though). Mr. Obama has just undermined their heroic efforts.

So the stimulus package finally passed. It's considerably less than what Mr. Obama wanted, thanks to the Republicans. Democrats love spending other people's money! And this stimulus package is the first step in becoming a Socialist nation. The U.S. government now has a 40% stake in some of the nation's largest banks. I said a long time ago that Liberalism equals Socialism. People have become so numb to what is going on. Everybody wants a hand-out and they are willing to give up their freedoms to get it.

The worst part of this stimulus is that our kids are going to be paying it back, plus interest. So while you are enjoying your little tax incentive now, your kids will be paying back three times as much later. Are you really proud of that? And when the government is providing your healthcare and your welfare check and whatever else it is you feel your entitled to, don't be surprised when you no longer have a Bill of Rights. Socialism is all encompassing. You can't have it in small doses. It's a virus. It spreads. It kills it's host and it permeates.

Socialism is for lazy people. People who work hard do not want the government in their business. The government wasn't set up to PROVIDE. It's function was to PROTECT.

Mr. Obama signed the Equal Pay Act. This may offend some women but oh well. Do I believe men and women should be paid equally? Yes. But only if they are doing EQUAL work. When they have to LOWER THE STANDARDS so that a woman can be a police officer or join the military, do I believe she should get the same pay? Absolutely not. In fact, she shouldn't even be in that line of work. We sacrifice quality and safety in the name of "equality". I'm sorry but women should not be police officers, fire fighters or military personnel…at least not in combat (which hasn't happened YET, thank God). Women are not physically as strong or able as men. Period. That's just the way it is. If you have a problem with that, take it up with God. Argue it with Him all you want. I guarantee you will lose. When I see women working construction or as police officers, I laugh. I know for a fact that they are NOT doing equal work. Are they trying just as hard as the men? Most likely. But they won't be able to do the same work. And therefore, should not receive equal pay. This bill is a joke. Just like Mr. Obama's Presidency so far.

Even worse than the Equal Pay Act is the Freedom of Choice Act he is so adamant about signing. This act will allow even MORE innocent babies to be murdered. It will repeal every piece of legislation currently in place that keeps abortion somewhat limited. It will make abortions available to anyone who wants one. Young girls will get abortions without parental consent. Wives will get abortions without consulting their husbands. There will be no limits. The sanctity of life is no more. For those of you that support abortion, I hope you also support Euthanasia. Your time is coming. You kills innocent babies now, but when that generation grows up, and they have no respect for life, don't be surprised when they want YOU out of the way when you are old and can't take care of yourself anymore.

It's a sad situation when we no longer respect an individual's right to life. It's sad when a woman's womb has become a combat zone. And Mr. Obama is looking to make abortions even more readily available. How do you think God will judge us for that?

I could go on and on about Mr. Obama but he really isn't worth any more of my time (not this month anyway!). I'm sure he will continue to lead us in the wrong direction. He is so adamant about the "rights" of terrorists in prison camps but he has no regard at all for unborn children.

Why couldn't Mike Huckabee have been our President???

Chapter Twelve:
Barack Hussein Obama Is President! Or–American Has Fallen and Can't Get Up

It's 11 o'clock in the morning and I'm watching CBS news and their extensive coverage of the Inauguration. I have to admit that it IS history in the making. America has come a long way from the days of slavery and even the days of segregation. I find it ironic that one day after Martin Luther King day we are inaugurating our first black President. I won't deny the significance of this.

However, the constant comparisons between Barack Obama and Abraham Lincoln are driving me crazy. The only thing Barack has in common with Abe is that they are/were both Senators from Illinois. (Is it ironic that Abe Lincoln was a Republican and he freed the slaves?). Beyond that, Barack isn't fit to tie Abe Lincoln's shoes.

Katy Couric has an annoying voice. I feel as though I'm going to break out into seizures at any moment. (Apparently Ted Kennedy feels the same way). Can someone just run their fingernails down a chalk board instead? Anyway, she mentions that Obama is going to use his middle name when inaugurated so as to "reach out" to Muslims. Is it just me or is the writing on the wall here? Should I just change my name to Muhammad now or wait until it becomes part of a stimulus package?

They are showing all the past Presidents now. Does Jimmy Carter really count? I think he's got a mouthful of peanuts...no...that was him talking. Sorry. It's amazing how good George Bush Sr. looks. However, the same cannot be said for Barbara Bush. Although she doesn't look any older than when she was the First Lady. But then again, is it POSSIBLE to look any older? No matter. She was a great First Lady and I guess that's what really matters. People are actually cheering for Bill Clinton. That's a pretty good indicator of the kind of people that voted for Obama. So much for morals and keeping America's national security, right?

They just showed Michelle Obama. She's pretty. She strikes a strange resemblance to Oprah. I'm not sure if that's good or bad. Even though she looks happy I can't help but remember her stating that it's only now that she is proud of her country. So much for patriotism. The only time she can be proud is when her husband is in power.

I like this Reverend Rick Warren. Obama caught some flack for having someone with morals being affiliated with him. Liberals don't like that. Morals make them queasy. Obama may be charged for treason amongst the other Liberals after the Inaugural Galas. I think Obama was pandering to Conservatives and Christians. He doesn't actually like this guy. Reverend Warren is pro-life and against gay marriage. No... Obama is trying to look as though he is "bi-partisan". You would have to be an idiot to actually believe this is sincere on Obama's part. Then again, there are close to 2 million people here...

There's no denying that Aretha Franklin has a beautiful voice and will always be the Queen of Soul. But she should lay off the ham sandwiches. Otherwise she's going to suffer the same fate as Mama Cass.

Question: if Barack is all about unity and bringing together white folks and black folks, how come he never acknowledges his white half? I can't help but recall when he referred to his grandmother as a "typical white person"...as though all white people are racist and scared of black people. Again, how does this guy get away with this stuff?

I just spotted Ted Kennedy! You know he's drunk! He's probably got a bottle of Scotch in his hand. Just don't let him drive in the motorcade. Especially if driving past a body of water.

Obama is taking his Oath now. I think he handled the little "mess up" rather well. I'll give him props for that. However, they aren't showing that his hand is actually on the Bible. They did a close up when Biden took his oath. I'm not saying anything…draw your own conclusions.

Obama is making his speech now. I have to admit that he is a great speaker. But then again so was Bill Clinton. He mentions how his goal is to stay true to the founding documents that have served our nation so well. Yet he is actually just like every other Liberal that claims that the Constitution is a "living document" and is subject to change. You know…like when you want to eliminate the Second Amendment.

Now he's talking about the entitlement of happiness and success. Sorry Barack but the "document" states the PURSUIT of happiness. Not the guarantee of happiness, nor of success. Typical Democrat. Everything should be a hand-out. He follows this up with "the question shouldn't be is the government too big or too small, but does it work?". Again, typical Democrat. Big government. Entitlements. The government is supposed to provide jobs and healthcare and everything else we want! This is the antithesis to Democracy and Capitalism. If you want everything handed to you then move to Canada.

Barack says the U.S. should be a friend to all nations. Even terrorist nations! He stated that he would open dialogue with all nations, including terrorist nations. Can you compromise our safety just a little bit more Mr. Obama…I'm still feeling a bit safe from George W's term…

I just spotted Colin Powel. Traitor. His vote for Obama was strictly a racial one. He has been a die-hard Republican for ages and then all of the sudden he switches sides? Why didn't he switch when Clinton was in office? Oh yeah…that's because, despite Bill's claim to being the first black President, Bill is white! (I'm sure most of you already knew that).

Oh boy…this is where Obama "talks tough". Democrats talking tough is like my grandmother lifting weights. Barack says (to al-Qaeda), "you cannot outlast us and we will defeat you!". And then he tucks his tail and withdraws all our troops out of Iraq. That'll show 'em! He will tear down everything Reagan, Bush and W. Bush worked so hard to establish. America will look weak and you will see terrorist attacks again. Let me remind you that under George W., we saw no further attacks after 9/11. How come that always somehow gets overlooked?

He's addressing his Muslim friends now. He promises to shop at 7-11 more frequently. What a nice guy!

Thank God his speech is over.

Wait...the inaugural "poet" is on now. Inaugural poet? I'm not sure which is more nauseating...Barack's speech or this lady's poem. Is this for real?? Is this proof that "Hooked On Phonics" *doesn't* work for everyone?

Reverend Joseph Lowery is giving the Benediction. Why doesn't someone get him something to stand on? He looks like my grandmother behind the wheel of her Buick.

Hey look! Barack is actually singing the National Anthem! I wonder why it suddenly appeals to him now? A year ago, a picture came out showing that he refused to sing and he refused to put his hand over his heart. And this guy is our President?

Well, it's all said and done now. Barack Hussein Obama is our 44th President. I will pray for him and pray that he makes better choices than the one's he has been adamant about. I try to remain optimistic but it's very hard to do so. I cannot feel confident about a man that supports abortion, stem cell research and gay marriage.

Maybe in 4 years America will wake up again and elect a Republican for President. And maybe Michael Moore will go on a diet too...

Chapter Thirteen:
Remember When America Was a Capitalist Democracy?

It's been awhile since the last issue of "Voice of Reason" came out and I do apologize for the delay. But a lot has happened so there's a lot to talk about.

My good pal Mark Haley once told me that when he was a kid he used to play basketball by himself and do the play-by-play commentary as well. Imagine that…Mark didn't have any friends (which isn't surprising if you've ever met this guy). But that is beside the point. The point is that this article will read like a "play-by-play" commentary only because I could write for weeks on Barrack Hussein Obama, so I have to keep it within suitable timelines.

Let's start with economics. Mr. Obama has already put us further in debt (to the Chinese no less) by about $1.3 trillion. You might be saying to yourself, "no, it's only $780 billion!" (As if there's a such thing as ONLY $780 billion). What you have to keep in mind is the interest that will have to be paid back. When you take that into consideration, it's $1.3 trillion.

Economics cannot be discussed without talking about the economy. Congress patted themselves on the back for passing a stimulus package that has accomplished only 2 things so far:

1. It's ok for the government to waste money and not hold themselves accountable. Who bails me out if I come up short on my car payment? No one. Congress applauds itself when it should be ashamed of itself. They should have had enough foresight to prevent this. They certainly should have enough accountability to not pass the burden of their errors on to the tax payer.

2. We now have a much larger national debt and we are further indebted to China. I don't know about you, but I'm not comfortable with owing Communist China money. Can someone say loan shark?

On top of all this, it came out a few weeks ago that the "growth" that resulted from the stimulus was greatly exaggerated. The numbers were so inflated that even members of Obama's administration had to admit they were far fetched. Unemployment has not decreased by much at all and inflation, if anything, is still rising.

What really gets me is that while Americans are struggling to make ends meet and find jobs, Obama wastes $328,000 to have a picture of Air Force One taken while in flight to put on his website. Then he spends $2,000 on a dog. He promised there would be no tax increase for the middle class but he's sneaky! Clinton has nothing on Mr. Obama! He didn't tax anyone directly but the cigarette tax primarily hit's the middle class. 86% percent of all smokers make less than $36,000 per year. He's gonna get ya one way or another!

And if *he* doesn't get you, the terrorists he released from Guantanamo Bay will!

People in the military put their lives on the line to keep America (and the rest of the world) free. Their efforts should not be in vain. But Obama doesn't care about that. He's more concerned with keeping the terrorists comfortable. And since Guantanamo Bay doesn't offer wi-fi and room service, it was inhumane to keep the terrorists locked up there. So now they roam around America and innocent American citizens are at risk.

Now to address what the title of this article hints at. We are quickly becoming a Socialist nation. You know what? If you want free government healthcare then move to Canada. This is America! It's a CAPITALIST DEMOCRACY!! If you don't like it or think it's unfair then move someplace where the government is set up to give hand-outs. Obama wants GM and Chrysler to be owned by the government. He wants the government to own the banks too. In fact, some banks are now primarily owned by the government. Obama even went so far as to fire the CEO of GM. What gives him that right? I thought stockholders made those decisions. Not only that, he wants to control the banks and decide how they conduct business. Do you not see the writing on the wall? To take it one step further, he even wants to control the banks that did NOT accept any bail-out money!

Granted, the banks acted very irresponsibly with their lending practices. You don't give someone a mortgage that's worth more than the home you're using as collateral. But again, who accepted the loans? Everyday Americans who wanted some easy money. So the American people are just as much to blame. No matter. The government should stay out of it. No bail-outs and certainly no government control. The government's job...listen carefully...is to build roads and keep us safe from foreign invasion. That's it. We, the people, wanted it that way. We want our personal freedoms and the opportunities that a capitalist democracy provides.

Speaking of government hand-outs, Mr. Obama is still trying to push his government mandated healthcare on everybody. Sara Palin was quoted recently as calling Obamacare "evil". I agree with her. You have to remember that your healthcare would be put entirely in the government's hands. They would decide what treatment you receive and IF you even deserve to get it. That's right...IF you DESERVE to get it. Liberals do not have morals. None. If you're a person with some sort of handicap or you are deemed a fiscal burden to society, you will not receive any healthcare. Liberals don't value life unless it's up to their standards. (Does the name Hitler sound familiar?)

Liberals already condone abortion and embryonic stem cell research so what makes you think they are going to value the life of someone with physical or mental impairments? Obamacare would also mandate that YOUR tax dollars be used to fund abortions and euthanasia. That's right...euthanasia.

Obama tries to tell us that those of us with our own private insurance will get to keep it. He's a liar. He's worse than Bill Clinton. Private insurance companies will not be able to compete with government provided insurance and they will fail. And then your only choice will be Obamacare. I understand that there are people without healthcare. But healthcare is not a right. It's not a given. It's not a guarantee. It's a privilege. And yes, it should be more readily available to the masses but it's not your God given right to have health insurance.

The issue of health care is not an easy fix. But it doesn't belong in the hands of the government. Health insurance is expensive and that's why a lot of employers don't offer it. But George W. Bush proposed an idea way back in 2004 that would have helped alleviate the financial burden of offering health care by smaller businesses. Obviously, the more you buy the less the cost. Simple economics (unless you're a Democrat). That's why large corporations can buy health care at much better prices. So George W. proposed letting smaller businesses band together and buy healthcare benefits. That way they would get the better prices that large businesses already enjoy. Think of it as a Sam's Club Blue Cross. Doesn't that make sense? But of course, the Democrats shot that down because then it would leave it in the hands of businesses and individuals. We can't have that! That would ruin any chances of turning the United States into a Socialist nation.

One last thing about Obamacare. It would also cover illegal aliens. That means your tax dollars would cover non-citizens, who are here ILLEGALLY, and who do not pay taxes. The crazy thing is that the people that are here illegally actually feel they are entitled to this. They complain because they don't already have it. Here's an idea: if you're unhappy with how things are done in America, then go home. Now. We don't need you and you don't belong here. If you want to live in America then do so legally and you will be welcomed with open arms and you will then have the right to complain. Until then: shut up and go home. I would never move to another country and expect them to give me healthcare when I don't pay taxes. Especially if I was there illegally. And I also wouldn't expect them to change their national language to English.

It's quite simple and common courtesy: if you want to live and work in America, learn to speak English. If I move to France and expect to live and work there, I will learn to speak French. That just makes sense.

Oh how I long for the days of Ronald Reagan. When America was strong. When America had morals. When America was a Capitalist Democracy.

Chapter Fourteen:
President Obama Talks Tough (and my grandma challenges Hulk Hogan to an arm wrestling match)

You know…my job as contributor to this newsletter keeps getting easier. I can almost do it my sleep. Obama is such an easy target. It's not even a challenge anymore. Of course, that doesn't make it any less fun to point out what a joke of a President he is!

In response to the missile that North Korea launched our steadfast President was so bold and courageous that he threatened to send a "stern" letter! I'm sure North Korea as a whole is shaking in fear! A stern letter?!? What's next…a sanction that will result in no Christmas card being sent this year!!?!?

North Korea has broken so many policies, treaties, etc with the launching of this missile that I'm not sure why immediate action isn't being taken. By the way, I mean REAL action. Not stern letters and mean looks. It's a no-brainer! Where is Ronald Reagan when we need him? In fact, George W. Bush would have handled this much better. Obama is intent on making America look weak and he is off to a great start. Not only has he set a withdrawal date in Iraq (which is an invitation for al-Qaeda) but now he is refusing to flex some muscle with North

Korea. Imagine what happens when North Korea starts selling their weapons to Iran. Oh yeah…that WILL happen. The Middle East will fall out of balance at that point and we will feel the repercussions.

On top of all this, Obama makes a trip to France and bad-mouths his own country, calling the United States "arrogant" and basically apologizing to those spineless traitors. What in the name of Dixie Chicks is going on here?!?! Obama is a traitor. He hates America and all it stands for. That's why the French like him so much. If the French like you, you're in trouble. Why would you want the French as an ally? I mean, do they really even count as an ally? Isn't the point in having an ally is so that someone has your back? Or have I been misinformed somewhere along the way. Not only did the French NOT back us in Iraq but they continued to sell weapons to our enemies!

It seems to me that Obama's foreign policy is just as deplorable as his domestic policy. And it's only going to get worse. If we still have a country in four years I pray to God that we elect a Republican who can re-establish us as the sole World Power. That may sound arrogant to Obama but to sane people it means security and protection from terrorists.

Isn't that the President's job???

Chapter Fifteen:
Mike Huckabee: 2012

Everyone is talking about this movie called 2012. I guess it's about the end of the world or something. Personally, I don't care for movies like that. No one but God knows when the end is coming so why dwell on it? Although, I do believe the end of the United States as we know it could very well be imminent. Mr. Obama (that's right...MISTER Obama) stands a very good chance of turning our country into a Godless, socialist nation.

But I don't want to focus too much on Mr. Obama right now. I want to talk about our one true hope for bringing greatness and Godliness back to our country. That one true hope is none other than Mike Huckabee. He should have been our President back in 2008 but unfortunately, there are too many people in this country that want entitlements. Wouldn't you know it that the one time the laziest of our population decides to get off their butts and do something, it would be election day?

No matter. Mr. Obama has been President for 11 months and really hasn't accomplished a whole lot. Which is good.

Mike Huckabee was governor of Arkansas for 12 years and in his time, he made numerous, significant changes. And he did it with a Democratic majority in both state houses. Now how could Huckabee get things done when he was clearly outnumbered but Mr. Obama can't get anything done even though the Democrats control both houses? That's a great question and I thank myself for asking it. Now you, the reader, get to reap the benefits of my insightful, and totally unbiased, answer.

First of all, Mr. Obama's agenda is so radically left-wing that even the Democrats call it liberal. Secondly, most people are happy with a Capitalist Democracy. They do not want to give up their freedom and rights and be subjected to a Socialist regime.

Mike Huckabee often refers to "Vertical Politics". I wasn't exactly sure of what that meant until I heard him speak about it. I have read 2 of his books so far and he goes in to great detail about what that means. In short, it's not about "Left wing" or "Right wing" (horizontal), it's about doing what is best for the majority. It means moving in an upward trajectory. That's why Huckabee was able to stay in office for so long in a state where it's almost a crime to be a Republican. Most people are concerned with what makes the country BETTER. The people of Arkansas, for the most part, didn't care that Huckabee was a Republican. They were concerned with how his policies affected the state he governed.

That's not to say that people are not concerned with party affiliation. Most of us align ourselves with the party that best represents our own sentiments. Those of us that have morals (sanctity of life, oppose gay marriage, etc) and have respect for what this country stands for (protecting the 2nd Amendment, establishing Democracy, etc) align ourselves with the Republican party. Those who hate America and wish that it would crumble and become an entitlement rich, socialist regime align themselves with the Democrats.

I strongly recommend that you read Mike Huckabee's newest book, "Do The Right Thing". You will agree that he is the best candidate for President, and certainly, our last hope to retain and reestablish what this country was founded on.

President Huckabee….I like the sound of that.

Chapter Sixteen:
For Real Americans Only

In the last issue of "The Voice of Reason" I briefly touched on the issue of illegal immigrants. In light of the Amnesty Bill that is currently being debated and endorsed by Democrats, including Mr. Obama, I felt it necessary to elaborate on that particular issue.

The question that seems to get debated over and over again is, "who is an American?". Those on the Left believe that anyone who lives here or immigrates here, whether legally or not, is an American. Those of us who are sane and actually use common sense and logic (we're on the Right by the way) believe those who live and immigrate here LEGALLY, are Americans. The current bill that is actually being considered would do the following:

-would give Amnesty (citizenship) to those who have immigrated here illegally
-would provide Health insurance to illegal immigrants
-would prevent back taxes from having to be paid but would offer tax credits and a period of tax-free exemption

All of this of course would be at YOUR expense. That means anyone who is a legal citizen would be paying to insure those who are here illegally. How can anyone in their right mind believe that this is fair? Democrats have absolutely no common sense. They champion all things that resemble Socialism. They claim to be looking out for the lower and middle class but then they raise taxes so that illegal immigrants can have better health insurance than working Americans have.

And who was a champion of these insane Amnesty bills? None other than Ted Kennedy. I am never happy when someone passes away, no matter how worthless and how much of an alcoholic he may have been. But let's not confuse longevity with statesmanship. Ted Kennedy was a Senator since the days of Moses and I really don't know what he ever accomplished (other than costing his state millions of dollars for the "Big Dig"). Everyone is talking about what a great man he was and what a true statesman he was. I guess if letting a young woman drown in your car due to your drunken stupor makes you a great man, then Ted Kennedy surely was just that! But I'm sure Ted spent plenty of time in jail for his crime right? Yeah…and his brother JFK was a faithful husband too.

Kennedy was one of those John Kerry types. He voted for the war in Iraq but when it became unpopular, tried to deny he ever voted for it. He then went on a campaign to end the war even though he voted for it! I'll never know how Kennedy stayed in office for so long. It has to be because he was from a liberal state. Had he been from Kansas or Iowa, he would have never had a career. In fact, Ted Kennedy is the very reason why there should be term limits on Senators and Representatives.

I have to say though, in a way I'm glad that Obama is in office. With all of his failed policies so far and the resistance he has met from the American people, I think when the next election comes up, people are going to be ready for real "hope and change". Obama's socialist health care has stalled because even the Democrats think that it goes too far. He is pushing to pass his evil legislation that would take abortion to a whole new level but I think the Republicans (and the American people) will put a stop to that. But even if he doesn't stand a chance of passing the Freedom of Choice Act, it's the principle that he actually TRIED. How can people vote for a man that has no regard for unborn children?

My point is that so far, thank God, all of the things he promised to do, haven't happened. And when you take into consideration that the Democrats control both houses, that's pretty pathetic.

But oh well...I'm smiling! Life is good. I honestly believe that Mr. Obama will be a one-term President. The Republicans have some strong contenders such as Newt Gingrich, Mike Huckabee and even Sara Palin. In fact, I think a Huckabee/Palin ticket would be very strong. At this point, I would take Carter/Mondale....well, maybe...

Until next time my fellow Americans!

Chapter Seventeen:
The Truth About
Barrack Hussein Obama

Far be it for me to tell anyone how to vote…unless you ask me of course. Actually, even if you don't ask me I will probably still tell you anyway. It's my responsibility as a patriotic American and as a Culture Warrior. If you believe in traditional values then you had better vote for John McCain. If you believe that the principles that which this great country was founded on are deeply flawed then you are a secular-progressive and I guess you'll probably vote for Barack Hussein Obama.

You're probably asking two questions right now: what is a Culture Warrior and what is the difference between a Traditionalist and a Secular-Progressive? Those are very good questions and I'm proud of you for asking!

Most people are familiar with the differences between Democrats and Republicans. Most people are familiar with the differences between liberals and conservatives. Typically speaking, Democrats tend to be liberal and Republicans tend to be conservative. That's not always the case (I.e. Reagan Democrats) but more times than not, it is. Traditionalists are conservative. Secular-Progressives are liberal. And right now America is at war with itself. (You can find even more about this in Bill O'Reilly's wonderful book, "Culture Warrior").

Secular-Progressives (SP's) are pro-choice, pro gay marriage, anti-religion and anti-George W. Bush. SP's are best represented by the ACLU (American Civil Liberties Union). Sounds patriotic right? It isn't. It's because of organizations like the ACLU that an underage girl has the right to have an abortion without getting consent from her parents. It's because of liberal SP's that abortion is even legal. It's also because of SP's that the phrase "separation of Church and State" exists. Which is a misnomer. All of our founding fathers were very religious. Every document from The Declaration to the Constitution is Biblically based. The very foundation of our country is based on Jewish/Christian belief and tradition. Yet the SP's want to take prayer out of school, the Ten Commandments out of public buildings and "one nation under God" out of the Pledge of Allegiance. I'm sure by now you have come to the conclusion that Traditionalists (such as I) stand for the exact opposite.

Traditionalists believe that, although the U.S. has certainly had it's share of stained history, for the most part America has stood for justice and equality. Never in history has a superpower not abused it's strength in hostile take-over of other nations. Traditionalists believe in the sanctity of life. Life begins at conception and therefore needs to be protected. Traditionalists believe that marriage is a union between one MAN and one WOMAN.

So what does all of this have to do with Barack Hussein Obama? He easily and most readily fits into the category of a liberal SP. He is for abortion. In fact, he believes that even if a baby survives an abortion and is born alive it should be legal to kill it. He is for gay marriage. And he has, on several occasions, mocked Christianity.

He claims to be a Christian yet he attended a Muslim school. He refuses to wear an American Flag pin on his lapel (Note: only recently has Obama started wearing the Flag on his lapel. Only now that he's a Presidential candidate will he wear one. No political motivation there!). He refuses to put his hand over his heart during the National Anthem. He belongs to a Church that is lead by Rev. Jeremiah Wright. Rev. Wright has been quoted as saying "God bless America? I say, God Damn America!". Rev. Wright is affiliated with Black Liberation

Theology which is the black equivalent to the KKK. This is who Barack Hussein Obama calls his "spiritual mentor". Let's not forget Barack's affiliation with William Ayers either. Ayers of course is a terrorist that blew up several government buildings during the 60's and 70's. Barack likes to claim that he can't help that he lives in the same neighborhood as Ayers. I agree. But he CAN avoid going to the man's house and shaking hands with him in his living room.

Barack Hussein Obama has been a Senator for less than 4 years. In that time he has voted "present" on over 100 issues! That means that on 100 separate occasions he refused to take a stand on issues. What kind of leadership is that? By the way, even Hillary Clinton and John Edwards confronted Obama on the Ayers issue and the voting issue during the primaries.

Speaking of Hillary…

Why didn't Obama take Hillary as his running mate? As much as I hate to admit it, it would have been a nearly unbeatable ticket. So why wouldn't he ask her to be his VP? It's quite simple. Ego. Barrack is so caught up in being the first black President that he wouldn't want to share the spotlight with the first female vice-president. Obama claims that he wants to "change" Washington yet he picks a Washington insider like Joe Biden for his running mate!

This is my favorite part…it's where we review what we've learned today. (With a few new tid-bits as well)…

-Obama is pro-choice

-Obama is for gay marriage

-Obama wants to destroy the Jewish/Christian foundation that this country is founded upon

-Obama wants to do away with the 2nd Amendment

-Obama never mentions the success we have had in Iraq

-Obama has stated that he will open talks with known Terrorist Nations

It seems to me that Obama wants to compromise our safety…all in the name of diplomacy. He is more concerned with our being accepted by other countries than with keeping Americans safe from terrorist attacks.

The most frightening aspect of radical liberals like Obama is their aspiration to turn America into a Socialist nation. They want to take away your Second Amendment rights and create more social programs at tax-payer expense. They are against the death penalty for murderers and rapists but they support and condone the brutal killing of millions of innocent babies.

People say they are against abortion and that they disagree with Obama's stance on the issue but they will vote for him anyway due to the economy. I ask: can you put a price tag on human life? Is a better economy worth the horrific truth of abortion? The economy takes care of itself. It goes in cycles. It WILL recover. It always does. When I stand before God someday I don't want to have to answer for voting for someone that supported abortion. "But it's ok God! It was for a better economy and lower gas prices!". Do you think He cares about that?

I find it hard to believe that people will actually vote for Obama. Then again, the media (liberally biased) has done nothing to tell us who Obama really is and what he really stands for. If people really knew what they were getting they might change their minds. Ignorance is NOT bliss people. I am a Culture Warrior and now you know why.

Here are some websites you might want to check out to learn about who Obama REALLY is:

www.eyeblast.com
www.exposeobama.com

Addendum:

Regarding Barack Hussein Obama's health care plan. If you choose NOT to have health insurance or if you are a small business that CANNOT provide health insurance, you will be FINED! And how much more do we want to put the government in control of? The Democrats, Barack Hussein Obama in particular, want to put health care in the greedy hands of the government! Again, this is NOT a socialist society! The government is supposed to have MINIMAL impact on our day to day lives.

As far as education goes…sure…Barack Hussein Obama wants to offer more scholarships and grants…but only if you're a minority. If you're a poor WHITE kid…too bad. That's what Affirmative Action does. Thank God it has been outlawed in Michigan.

You see…there is always a catch when the Democrats start talking about "helping the middle class". It usually applies only to certain groups and it ends up costing EVERYONE more in taxes. Big government: it's the antithesis to Democracy and Capitalism.

Chapter Eighteen:
America Desperately Needs A Doctor (and a whole lot of prayer too)

As I sit here typing this, the reality of what happened on November 4 still hasn't set it. It might take some time. I'm sure when January 20, 2009 rolls around, some of you will witness me crying for the first time in over 15 years. There goes my streak. By the way, the last time I cried was when I watched "Return of the Jedi" and Darth Vader died. I'm not sure what to even think or feel at this point. I cannot imagine why anyone would vote for Obama. Other than the usual reasons of wanting more welfare checks, I don't know why anyone would want Obama for President.

I watched the election results as they came in. I couldn't believe what was happening. And of course, the liberally biased media was in their prime! They were having a field day with this! And all anyone could talk about was what a "moment in history" this was. "The first African-American President". No one wanted to mention what a horrible position we are in now! Joe Biden, before being named Obama's running mate, had stated, "I guarantee that within 6 months of Obama taking office, their will be a terrorist attack on our country". The media was so caught up in "historical moments" that the fact that we are going to be attacked sometime in the next four years, somehow seemed trivial!

Great…I'll get bombed with a black President in office rather than a white President. Lucky me! But hey…let's make history!

In the last issue of The Voice of Reason, I gave you a lot of reasons as to why you shouldn't vote for Obama. Apparently some of you didn't listen. So this month I'm going to tell what you can now expect:

-for those of you that fell for that whole "tax break" for the middle class stuff…first of all, rescind your right to vote so we won't have to deal with you again. Thanks. Secondly, don't expect the tax break. There is NO WAY Obama can give a tax break and still fund all his favorite Socialist, hand-out programs. So if you voted for a "tax break", don't hold your breath. What WILL happen is that Obama is going to heavily tax small businesses so much that most of them will have to shut down. Small businesses create more jobs than all large corporations. You do the math. That means loss of jobs. Large corporations that face huge increases will simply move to other countries where the taxes are much lower. What does that mean? Loss of jobs!

-for those of you who think you're going to get free health-care, please renounce your citizenship and move to Canada. There is no such thing as FREE! Everything has to be paid for somehow, some way. Small businesses will be forced to provide health-care or shut down. Most will shut down because they can't afford it. Or they will have to cut wages to afford paying for health-care. Again, loss of jobs and/or loss of wages. For families that can't afford the "mandatory" health-care, they will be fined! Now…if a family can't afford health-care, how will they afford the fine?

-for those of you that think Obama will bring an "honorable" end to the war in Iraq…do you not realize that pulling out of Iraq will cause instability in the Middle East? We have made great progress there but the work is not done! If we leave now, all our progress will be lost. Not to mention that it will make us look weak, opening the door for more terrorist attacks. Let us not forget: under the Bush Administration there have been no terrorist attacks since 9/11. The men and women in Iraq are there because THEY SIGNED UP TO SERVE IN THE MILITARY! IT'S THEIR JOB! There is no draft. They are there because they chose to be. If they wanted to come home and leave the job unfinished, then why do a huge majority of military personnel vote Republican? Obama WILL cut military spending. Our military will suffer and so will our security. Think I'm wrong? Think back to the Clinton administration and the cuts he made.

-for those of you who expect that Obama is going to rescue the economy…you are delusional at best. Not to mention that the economy is SUPPOSED to go in cycles. It is supposed to be bad sometimes. The President has little effect on the economy. With all the taxation he will implement how does he expect it to stimulate the economy? The bad economy has been good for me! I like paying $2.09 a gallon for gas as opposed to $4.00 per gallon! Above all that, is a good economy worth Obama's stance on abortion? Or his goal of eliminating the Second Amendment? How do you justify voting for Obama's "better economy" knowing his horrific stance on abortion?

-you CAN expect that abortion will become more prominent. Obama will be appointing justices to the Supreme Court. Do you think they will be conservative judges? They will be as liberal as he is.

-you can also expect for your right to bear arms to be heavily challenged. For those of you that like to hunt or, I don't know…protect your family! You can expect to lose that right. Or come close anyway.

I could go on forever as to why this country made a horrible choice. Not to mention that the moral decline in this country has rapidly accelerated. We are getting to the point of being as Godless as Europe. I still love my country and I will pray for Obama and the Democratically controlled Congress. But I think we all better realize now that the next 4 years are not going to be easy. It will be a trying time for conservative Americans with traditional Christian values. The fact that Proposal 2 passed is in an indication of deplorable moral and ethical values. Using embryos for experimentation? Remember, life begins at conception. That is fact. So you are ending one life to MAYBE save another? Who made you God? I can't even imagine what will come of this. You will see other things come out of this. Next it will be cloning. Then it will be creating a person solely to take his/her organs for other people. Disposable life. It will happen.

It was a pivotal election and unfortunately, the good guys lost. John

McCain did as well as any Republican could possibly do. It was an uphill battle when you consider the low approval rating of George Bush (although the Democratically controlled Congress has an even LOWER approval rating), the economy and the war in Iraq. McCain was very gracious in his concession speech. He spoke like a true American... because HE is one. His speech was much better than Obama's tried and true (albeit very tiring and predictable) "hope and change" spin. Obama is good at telling people what they want to hear. McCain actually has the experience, integrity and PATRIOTISM to do what is best for his country. We now have a President that will not put his hand over his heart for the National Anthem, has ridiculed the Bible, belonged to a Black Supremacist church for 20 years and is intent on making this a Socialist nation. And yet he says he loves his country? Why would anyone want this kind of person as the leader of our nation?

I'm anxious to see what awaits us over the next 4 years...

God Bless America.

Chapter Nineteen:
Where Have All The Cowboys Gone?

Americans used to stand up for what they believed in. We have become a bunch of apathetic zombies, content with our fast-food, reality TV shows and 24 hour Wal-Marts. Meanwhile, the government keeps growing bigger and our individual freedoms continue to dwindle. We're like cattle being lead to slaughter.

Obama has endorsed the building of a Mosque at Ground Zero. This doesn't surprise me at all considering that Obama is a Muslim and hates America. What does surprise me is that 90% of the population doesn't agree with it, but is too caught up in watching Oprah to do anything about it. Building a Mosque a Ground Zero is the ultimate slap in the face to anyone who remembers what happened on September 11, 2001. It's the equivalent of going to a Jewish temple and hanging up Nazi symbols.

And now we are pulling out of Iraq. How long do you think it will take before al-Qaeda moves in and takes over? The most basic principle of war is to not let the enemy know what your next move is. Yet Obama makes an announcement as to when we will be leaving and what flight number we will be on. Why not just send the terrorists an invitation?

How soon we forget. We are tucking our tails and running. Do you realize how weak that makes us look? The job was not finished. We set out to destroy al-Qaeda because of the 5,000 innocent lives they destroyed and instead we are making it easier for them to launch yet another attack on us. It's the government's fault alright. But the American people are no better. There were people in the streets protesting when we first invaded Iraq…and this was right after 9/11! The Obama administration continues to impose it's socialistic policies on us and Americans keep turning the other cheek.

Here's another example of how apathetic Americans have become. Pepsi recently released a commemorative can with the Pledge of Allegiance on them. Only they left out the "under God" part. Their reasoning was that they didn't want to "offend" anyone. Well, they offended me! And what about every other Christian American that was offended? I have since boycotted all Pepsi products. Will it affect Pepsi in any way? Probably not. But at least I can sleep at night. "As for me and my house, we will serve the Lord."

I'm hoping that Americans will not forget their outrage when Congress elected to pass a Health Care bill that over half of the population did not want. People were angry and I hope that carries over to the November elections. Only with a Republican majority in both Houses can we start the process of overturning ObamaCare. The Obama administration is turning up the heat in trying to sell this to the public. They now have Andy Griffith doing commercials trying to convince people that socialism is a better way of life. I love Andy Griffith. The Andy Griffith Show is my favorite show of all time. I own all 8 seasons on DVD. I always admired his Christian music and I own several of his CD's. But how can he be a Christian and support a Health Care package that supports abortion, embryonic stem cell research and euthanasia? Every Christian bookstore should be taking his books and CD's off their shelves. I understand that bookstores make money by selling books. But I'm curious to see if these Christian bookstores value something more than making money.

The most disturbing example of American apathy is the birth certificate issue. The fact remains that Obama has yet to disclose his long form birth certificate. I have to disclose my birth certificate to obtain a passport. I have to present my son's birth certificate so he can attend school. But Obama isn't required to show his birth certificate to be President? The Constitution clearly dictates that the President must be a natural born citizen. Obama is not. That is why he continues to avoid the issue. Do Americans not realize (or perhaps, they simply do not care) that our President is NOT an American citizen? Why aren't we pressing this issue? Why aren't the Republicans demanding that his birth certificate be shown? I will cut everyone some slack here because it's not just apathy that keeps us from pressing the issue. The other reason is because you will be labeled as racist. In fact, if you disagree with Obama in any way, shape or form, you must be racist. It's the favorite calling card for the Democrats right now. That's why they ran Obama in the first place. He was a Junior Senator with no experience whatsoever! Why else would they run him? It's because they could play the race card. And it obviously worked because he is now our President.

My last rant hits a little closer to home. When ObamaCare was about to be voted on, Bart Stupak announced that he would not be voting for it because his constituents did not support the federal funding of abortions. I thought that I could finally call a Democrat admirable! But a ride on Air Force One and a few special favors later, Stupak changed his mind and voted for ObamaCare anyway. Despite the fact that his constituents were adamant that he shouldn't. Stupak knew he had betrayed the people of Michigan and resigned from office shortly thereafter. He knew he had committed political suicide. But it just goes to show that politicians, Democrats in particular, talk about how they represent their constituents, but in reality they are in office to promote their own personal agendas. The only time politicians listen is during voting season and through campaign contributions. Any other time, they just want you to go away.

What happened to the America that stood for what was right? When men were men and women were women. When marriage was between a man and a woman? People lay down and allow the government to tread all over their Constitutional rights. We have no cowboys that will stand up and say "enough is enough!" We don't have any John Waynes that will fight for what they believe in. Americans have lost their backbone. We are moments away from becoming a socialist nation. Moments away from losing our personal liberties. Moments away from losing all that our ancestors fought for.

Closing Thoughts

I was too young to truly appreciate the Presidency of Ronald Reagan. I remember seeing him on TV and listening to him speak. But again, I was too young to really understand or appreciate what he was saying. I was too young to realize what he was doing for our country.

President Reagan was a champion of personal freedoms. He embraced liberty and gave our country a breath of fresh air. Morality reigned anew and Americans felt *safe*. For me it's history. For many it was an awakening. It's similar to an out-of-body experience for me. I was there but I wasn't really *there*. I look back on it now and have a greater appreciation for it. I have nostalgic feelings for it because our country has regressed so much since the days of Ronald Reagan.

Most of us hope to leave the country in better shape than which we received it. And for the most part I think that, historically, that has been true. However, I feel that we are leaving our children with an almost irreversible mess.

Mr. Obama has taken our country down so many wrong roads that I'm afraid we may never find our way again. He has taken the greatest country on Earth and made a mockery of it. America was a beacon of Democracy and now it has become a test-subject for neo-Socialism. It's disheartening to me to think that my son will never experience the freedoms and liberties that I have enjoyed.

Americans need to stand up and take their country back. Most Americans feel powerless but there is strength in numbers. You can make a difference at the polls. And even if all hope seems to be lost, just remember:

With God all things are possible.

Special Thanks

Where does one even begin when you try to thank all the people that have made an impact on your life? I guess I will start at the "beginning"…

First and foremost, I thank God for loving me unconditionally and continually blessing me in more ways than I could ever deserve. Secondly, I thank Jesus for making my path to Heaven so much easier. He continues to forgive even as I continue to fall short of His glory.

I thank my parents and step-parents for putting up with me…even to this day. I was never rebellious but always demanding. They had their work cut out for them.

I thank my sisters, Farrah and Nikki, who had to put up with my cruel pranks and aggravation. But hey…what are brothers for! It was my job to make their lives miserable and I think I deserve a raise!

To my step-sister Shannon: I thank you for motivation. There was a time when I wandered aimlessly and you showed me that hard work and dedication sometimes meant doing an unpleasant job.

My step-brother Jason gets props for being one of the meanest bass players around. He and I used to play in bands in high school and we were awful. Just being honest. But we have both come a long way and I appreciate that he helped me to get some of my original songs recorded in his studio. If you're looking to record a demo be sure to look him up.

I thank my maternal grandparents for allowing me to spend so much time with them. My grandmother would always make me eggs for breakfast and somehow they always tasted better when SHE made them! And my grandfather who would play his guitar which in turn inspired me to learn to play.

My paternal grandparents by far are responsible for my religious upbringing. They would read their Bibles every evening and then my grandfather would lead us in conversation. They also influenced my political interests as well, even though they were Democrats. But they were hard-core traditionalists and conservatives. The Democrats of that time are far different than the Democrats we have now. My grandparents are proof of that.

My best friends, Jon and Dave, whom I have known since high school. We have been tormenting anyone and everyone since day one and it still continues to this day! We take great pleasure in making others laugh…usually at themselves. They are my best friends now and forever.

To my great buddy Mark who has a wicked sense of humor and can impersonate just about anyone. He is the guy I have the most political conversations with and although we don't always agree, he is a fellow Christian, rightwing, conservative Republican.

To my friend Jamie, better known as Hookie-Lau, I owe a great deal of gratitude for teaching me to exhibit patience. She's a great listener too. And she puts up with my sense of humor even when she doesn't always get it!

To my friend Carla who is also a great listener and one of the most laid-back people I have ever met. She's a great pal even though she refuses to acknowledge that Trident is the best gum ever!

My friend Drew, whom I know through work. Although it is hard to forgive you for being a Democrat and even harder to forgive you for voting for Obama, I still remember all the great times we had on the old "South Unit". It will never be repeated but at least we have some great videos!

To George, Dawn and Linda…you are great people to work for. It's nice to finally work in an environment where I am at Liberty to speak about Jesus. Working for Christians has it's definite advantages.

My good friend Steve Shafer who provided me with one of the best interviews for my newsletter, "The Voice of Reason". Your crude humor, although sometimes borderline scary, is a refreshing breath of honesty!

To Tara…although we don't always get along, you're a great mom and you do a great job with our son. And to Kyle who is a great big-brother…Monster loves you!

To my nieces, Olyvia, Taylor and Ayla…I don't get to see you as much as I used to. I need to make a greater effort to do so.

To my kitty, Pumyra, who kept me company through my days of being single. She is loyal cat and has the prettiest eyes ever!

To my new pets, Gotto and Shandi…Pumyra doesn't like you but deep down I think she still loves you!

Ashleigh, Jalyn, Alec and Olivia…I'm glad that you are now a part of my life. I look forward to strengthening my relationship with you. Jalyn: you are an awesome athlete and I look forward to seeing you on the basketball court! If I can only keep the boys away from you! Alec: I am impressed with the 180 you have made in school this year! You are doing great! Olivia: you're going to be a looker someday! You're a sweet girl and a smarty pants! Ashleigh: I don't get to see you much but you're no less important to me. I hope I can see you again soon!

And to my Monster…you're a smart boy and a tough guy too! I'm proud to see that you have inherited my sense of humor…I just hope you don't inherit my hairline. Remember that I will always be proud of you…so long as you always vote Republican!

To Nicky…you are a God-send. You are patient and kind, and you love me for who I am…which isn't easy. You put up with my impatience and my ramblings about things you really don't care about. You attended a KISS concert with me even though you were skeptical. I thank you for everything that you are. And now you're a KISS fan so that makes you even more lovable! I love you forever…

Other influences in my life include Hulk Hogan (the training, the prayers and the vitamins…Hulk STILL Rules!), KISS (Gene and Paul especially), Bill O'Reilly, Elvis (the King!), the ThunderCats (truth, justice, honor and loyalty), Ann Coulter, Rush Limbaugh, Ronald Reagan, George W. Bush, Richard Nixon, Pastor Chris, Pastor Dave, Sarah Palin, Mike Huckabee, Rod Stewart, Knight Rider, The Dukes of Hazzard, Alex P. Keaton, Stryper, Quiet Riot, Motley Crue, Count Chocula, FrankenBerry and Boo Berry.

I also want to thank anyone and everyone who gave this book a chance. If you bought this book I hope you feel it was money well spent. I appreciate your support. I hope that in this great big political realm where "big name" politicians usually have the forum, a guy from the mid-west who is a virtual unknown, can also have a voice. I love my country and all that it stands for.

One nation, under GOD, indivisible…with liberty and justice for ALL.

www.ingramcontent.com/pod-product-compliance
Lightning Source LLC
Chambersburg PA
CBHW020346290526
45785CB00005B/2171